Childfree

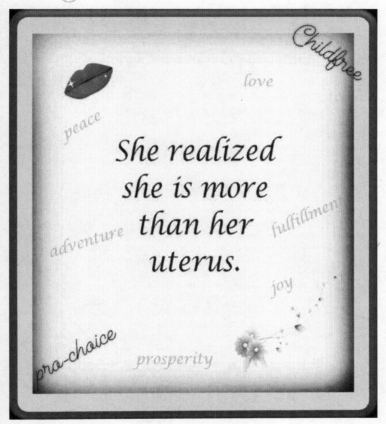

Childfree

love

peace

She realized
she is more
than her
uterus.

adventure

fulfillmen

joy

pro-choice

prosperity

I grew up reading The Baby-Sitters Club series.

I was going to name my future daughter after Claudia. I thought she was the coolest. Addicted to junk food and always had candy hidden around her room.

I had no idea motherhood was a choice.

No worries if you stare at the blank pages in this journal.

You don't have to write anything.

You can make a grocery list.

Trace your middle finger and write down the name of the person who pisses you off.

~LeNora Faye

Childfree

Love

adventure

Peace

Childfree

Love

adventure

Peace

Childfree

Love

adventure

Peace

Childfree

Love

adventure

Peace

Childfree

Love

adventure

Peace

Childfree

Love

adventure

Peace

Childfree

Love

adventure

Peace

Childfree

Love

adventure

Peace

Childfree

Love

adventure

Peace

Childfree

Love

adventure

Peace

Childfree

Love

adventure

Peace

Childfree

Love

adventure

Peace

peace

joy

Move along,
nothing to see here.

prosperity   adventure

Just a childfree woman
living her life.

love

fulfillment

Music kept me occupied as a child.

I began teaching violin at 15 and found myself too busy to attend regular high school.

I had dreams of building a large teaching practice and performing professionally.

I figured a husband and child would appear on my doorstep one day and I'd have to take care of them.

The summer I graduated, five of my friends got married.

I left home to attend college and to work for a community orchestra.

Life so far has been full of expected and unexpected adventures. All without having kids.

You may not know if you want kids.

The best thing you can do is explore what you love. See where it leads. Enjoy as much as you can. The answers come naturally with time.

~LeNora Faye

Childfree

Love

adventure

Peace

Childfree

Love

adventure

Peace

Childfree

Love

adventure

Peace

Childfree

Love

adventure

Peace

Childfree

Love

adventure

Peace

Childfree

Love

adventure

Peace

Childfree

Love

adventure

Peace

Childfree

Love

adventure

Peace

Childfree

Love

adventure

Peace

Childfree

Love

adventure

Peace

Childfree

Love

adventure

Peace

Childfree

Love

adventure

Peace

Childfree

The most empowering
moment for me
as a woman

was when I realized

I didn't have to become a
mother.

I was 22 years old when I had the epiphany that I didn't *have* to have kids.

My mother had recently died, and my 19-year-old brother announced he had gotten his ex-girlfriend pregnant.
It wasn't the greatest year of my life.

One afternoon, I stopped by the family home to visit with my dad.

I was sitting on the kitchen floor petting the dog when I said,

"I don't want to have children."

My dad told me I didn't have to.

Having the support of even one person in your life is priceless.

But sometimes all you have is yourself.

Journaling plays an important role in my daily life.
You can discover solutions as you vent your frustrations.

Or by doodling while listening to music.

~LeNora Faye

Childfree

Love

adventure

Peace

Childfree

Love

adventure

Peace

Childfree

Love

adventure

Peace

Childfree

Love

adventure

Peace

Childfree

Love

Peace

adventure

Childfree

Love

adventure

Peace

Childfree

Love

adventure

Peace

Childfree

Love

adventure

Peace

Childfree

Love

adventure

Peace

Childfree

Love

adventure

Peace

Childfree

Love

adventure

Peace

Childfree

Love

adventure

Peace

Childfree

HONESTY

Some people go through life not using their brain.

Why can't I go through life not using my uterus???

16 years old- I spent part of the summer at a youth leadership camp and then went to stay with family friends.

My relationship with my parents was at an all-time low, so any excuse to leave the house.

I stayed with a couple who had 3 little kids. This couple got married young. They bet me I would be married before I turned 25.

I'm 36 right now and unmarried.

Someone owes me a steak dinner.

I had the opportunity to be married at 25. Instead, I quit teaching, packed up my life as I knew it, and headed out on an adventure.

I discovered that my life has more than one career, more than one sexual position, and more than one path to fulfillment.

~LeNora Faye

Childfree

Love

adventure

Peace

Childfree

Love

adventure

Peace

Childfree

Love

adventure

Peace

Childfree

Love

adventure

Peace

Childfree

Love

adventure

Peace

Childfree

Love

adventure

Peace

Childfree

Love

adventure

Peace

Childfree

Love

adventure

Peace

Childfree

Love

adventure

Peace

Childfree

Love

adventure

Peace

Childfree

Love

adventure

Peace

Childfree

Love

adventure

Peace

Childfree

Parenting doesn't interest me

Parenting does **not** look fun.

I enjoyed being a teacher and I love being an aunt. It truly takes a village to raise a child.
But the daily life of a parent doesn't speak to me at all.

There are moments in life when it seems like nothing is happening.

Patience isn't my virtue.

But I don't wish to create a human being just so I have something to keep me busy for 20 years.

I have a nephew who loves to swim so I take him to the wave pool whenever he visits me. I use this opportunity to infiltrate the parenting world for a couple hours.

The things I hear in the hot tub...

~LeNora Faye

Childfree

Love

adventure

Peace

Childfree

Love

adventure

Peace

Childfree

Love

adventure

Peace

Childfree

Love

adventure

Peace

Childfree

Love

adventure

Peace

Childfree

Love

adventure

Peace

Childfree

Love

adventure

Peace

Childfree

Love

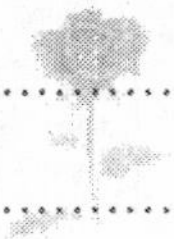

adventure

Peace

Childfree

Love

adventure

Peace

Childfree

Love

adventure

Peace

Childfree

Love

adventure

Peace

Childfree

Love

adventure

Peace

Childfree

adventure

prosperity

Childfree
doesn't mean
meaningless

love

joy

peace

fulfillment

It makes me giggle that I've found meaning in
sharing my desire to NOT be a mother.

Childfree

Who gets to decide what's meaningful and what
isn't?

Love

Oh wait, you do!

Because it's your life.

I've found meaning in creating a nice home for
myself. I don't mean the actual house, although I
love that too.

adventure

What I refer to is the vibe of my homelife.

It's peaceful, creative, non-judgemental. A safe
*Peace*space where I can be myself.

This is meaningful.

~LeNora Faye

Childfree

Love

adventure

Peace

Childfree

Love

adventure

Peace

Childfree

Love

adventure

Peace

Childfree

Love

adventure

Peace

Childfree

Love

adventure

Peace

Childfree

Love

adventure

Peace

Childfree

Love

adventure

Peace

Childfree

Love

adventure

Peace

Childfree

Love

adventure

Peace

Childfree

Love

adventure

Peace

Childfree

Love

adventure

Peace

Childfree

Love

adventure

Peace

peace   *adventure*   *love*

She doesn't have to
be a mother

to be a good lover
to be a good partner
to be a good friend
to be a good daughter
to be a good sister
to be a good aunt

to be a valuable member of
society.

prosperity

joy   *fulfillment*

I feel the burn in my throat when someone tells me I may regret not having kids.

I've turned that burn into a blog. And this journal.

An inspired FUCK YOU to the huddled masses. I say this with all the love in the world.

Finding your voice and acknowledging how you feel is **powerful**.

At this age, I don't regret my decision.

Life has shown me ways to feel fulfilled and enjoy my days beyond my imagination.

The darkness is always lurking, but I focus on the good.

Unless someone brings their baby to the theater and it's not a kid's movie. Then I get annoyed.

~LeNora Faye

Childfree

Love

adventure

Peace

Childfree

Love

adventure

Peace

Childfree

Love

adventure

Peace

Childfree

Love

adventure

Peace

Childfree

Love

adventure

Peace

Childfree

Love

adventure

Peace

Childfree

Love

adventure

Peace

Childfree

Love

adventure

Peace

Childfree

Love

adventure

Peace

Childfree

Love

adventure

Peace

Childfree

Love

adventure

Peace

Childfree

Love

adventure

Peace

Childfree

Wealth

Prosperity

Health

peace

love

She won't
procreate
just to
fit in.

joy

adventure

I've never fit in anywhere.

I'm biracial — born to a white mother and a black father. I grew up in white communities.

I was raised in a religion that has no name. I didn't have a TV or celebrate holidays.

I did gym class in a dress until 3rd grade. I told my mom I was flashing my underwear while doing the high jump. She finally bought me pants to change into at school.

In my 20s, I didn't relate to most people my age. I wasn't looking to be married with children.

In a way, all of this made me stronger in navigating through life as a childfree woman.

It's so nice when I do connect with someone else who doesn't want kids.

Once I felt comfortable enough to talk about my decision, a community of other childfree people appeared.

~LeNora Faye

Childfree

Love

adventure

Peace

Childfree

Love

adventure

Peace

Childfree

Love

adventure

Peace

Childfree

Love

adventure

Peace

Childfree

Love

adventure

Peace

Childfree

Love

adventure

Peace

Childfree

Love

adventure

Peace

Childfree

Love

adventure

Peace

Childfree

Love

adventure

Peace

Childfree

Love

adventure

Peace

Childfree

Love

adventure

Peace

Childfree

Love

adventure

Peace

Childfree

"Just wait until you have kids."

Me:

Wait for what?

I'm too busy living,
thanks.

I take things literally.

My dad always used this saying "nose to the grindstone", which means 'work hard'.
One time, I saw an actual grindstone in a museum.
Guess what? I put my nose to it and turned the handle.

Ouch!

I was 9 years old.

When someone says: "Wait until you have kids",
I think to myself
No, I'm not waiting for anything.

Parenthood is a choice!
If you want to create/raise a human to love and nurture, fine.

It's completely OK if you **don't** want to.

Give yourself time to discover all that you can be in this world.

~LeNora Faye

Childfree

Love

adventure

Peace

Childfree

Love

adventure

Peace

Childfree

Love

adventure

Peace

Childfree

Love

adventure

Peace

Childfree

Love

adventure

Peace

Childfree

Love

adventure

Peace

Childfree

Love

adventure

Peace

Childfree

Love

adventure

Peace

Childfree

Love

adventure

Peace

Childfree

Love

adventure

Peace

Childfree

Love

adventure

Peace

Childfree

Love

adventure

Peace

She won't regret exploring her childfree potential.

I dream big.

Sometimes, an idea appears in my head and I go 'WTF am I supposed to do with that?'

That's how The Bitchy Bookkeeper was created.

The name kept appearing in my head until I did something about it.

My most recent inspired dream involves creating a Vegas-style show. I'm still trying to wrap my brain around that one.

Something involving a one-woman monologue and playing the piano & violin. Plus, laser lights.

I've begun to write an hour-long script. And to practice my violin again.

I need to buy a piano.

So, dream big.

Have some fun in the process. Even if the dream changes, at least you'll have stories to tell.

~LeNora Faye

Childfree

Love

adventure

Peace

Childfree

Love

adventure

Peace

Childfree

Love

adventure

Peace

Childfree

Love

adventure

Peace

Childfree

Love

adventure

Peace

Childfree

Love

adventure

Peace

Childfree

Love

adventure

Peace

Childfree

Love

adventure

Peace

Childfree

Love

Peace

adventure

Childfree

Love

adventure

Peace

Childfree

Love

adventure

Peace

Childfree

Love

adventure

Peace

Childfree

Love

adventure

Peace

Childfree

Love

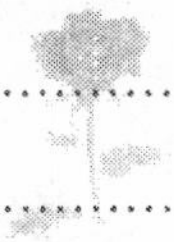

adventure

Peace

Childfree

Love

adventure

Peace

Childfree

Love

adventure

Peace

Childfree

Love

adventure

Peace

Childfree

Love

adventure

Peace

Childfree

Love

adventure

Peace

Childfree

Love

adventure

Peace

Childfree

peace

love

Your worth as a human being isn't tied to the number of kids you have.

fulfillment

joy

adventure

prosperity

Yay! You've made it to the end.

Or just skimmed through to read all the stories. Ha!

Childfree I won't judge.

I do hope you enjoyed your Bitchy Bookkeeper
Journal experience. *Love*

I'm having a lot of fun creating these. It begins with
an idea. And then, when the idea becomes reality
and you can hold it in your hand, it's like

OMG, I did it.

Now what?!

That's always the big question. Deep breath. What
can be done right now? *adventure*

Sometimes, the answer is NOTHING.

Perks of being childfree.... sometimes you get to do
nothing.

Peace

Until next time,

LeNora Faye

Made in the USA
Columbia, SC
01 June 2021